4/51   12/6

# ENGLISH VILLAGES

*in Pictures*

DUNSFORD, DEVONSHIRE

# ENGLISH
# VILLAGES

## *in Pictures*

INTRODUCTION BY BRIAN VESEY-FITZGERALD

CONTENTS

\*

ODHAMS PRESS LTD.     LONG ACRE, LONDON

## RUNSWICK BAY, YORKSHIRE

BETWEEN Whitby and Saltburn, Runswick clings to the cliff-side where the heather-covered North York Moors break abruptly at the sea. A tiny self-sufficient fishing community, Runswick probably had its origin during the Viking invasions of England's north-east coast. Later the working of jet into ornaments and charms was added to fishing as part of its people's livelihood. Like most other Yorkshire coastwise villages, it attracts further revenue from a large number of summer visitors by catering for holiday-makers.

# Introduction

"EVERY VILLAGE," said Thomas Hardy, "has its idiosyncrasy, its constitution." There are thirteen thousand and eleven villages in England (that figure does not include Scotland or Wales, nor does it include hamlets), and Thomas Hardy's statement is true of each one of them. Most English villages are very very old in their situations and in their shapes and in their names. All of them came into being to fulfil a particular purpose and were situated as they are for that precise reason. Yet each one is different, each has, too, its own personality. But that, it seems to me, is not the most important thing about English villages. The really important thing is not that they are all different, but that they all have one thing in common. It is this one common factor that is of supreme importance, for it is vitality. Both as a whole and in the individual details that go to their making English villages belong to the past and to the present.

It was the Saxons who brought the village to England. Of course, there were rural communities before the Saxons came to England; indeed, before the Roman conquest there was very little else. But the hill-top communities of pre-Roman Britain were not villages so much as camps.

It is often said that the word "village" came from the Roman villa. I do not myself believe that there is any close connexion between the two. If you must have a derivation, then I would suggest that the word comes from *vill*, which is a legal word for a number of houses with their lands, situated more or less closely together, and under a common organization. It is that word "organization" that is important. It is a common organization that makes a village no less than a town. There was no organization in this sense in pre-Roman Britain, and none in rural Britain during the Roman occupation. It was the Saxons with their valley cultivation who organized villages, and, broadly speaking, they did so in the first instance in order to make more easy the cultivation of the land. There are some exceptions to this rule, but not many. In the normal run of English villages the site has obviously been very carefully chosen with a view to economy of labour, with a view to saving the men who worked the land—and especially the ploughmen—unnecessary physical effort. It was this consideration that has, for the most part, given to English villages the shape they retain to this day. (In the few exceptions—and there are really surprisingly few—defence was the overriding consideration, and these few villages can easily be recognized by their situations and by their shape, which is nearly always roughly circular.)

It is a most extraordinary thing that the English villages should to so great an extent have retained the shape laid down for them so long ago. There have, of course, been accretions with the passing of years, but these have nearly always been on the outside, on the edge, and the observant eye can still pick out the original plan with little difficulty. Indeed, this is true even in many of those villages that have since grown into towns. It really is an extraordinary thing, for consider the changes that have been wrought in rural England since Saxon times.

The break-up of the manorial system, which meant the creation of farmers and yeomen and copyholders: the rise and fall of sheep-farming: the enclosures, first of the sixteenth century and then of the eighteenth: the intensive wheat-farming of the mid-nineteenth century: the return from corn to grass: the great agricultural depressions: the wrecking of the great estates: these are but a few of the more important changes. Each should have been sufficient to destroy the village organization. The village has survived them all. It has done so because all through the ages it has sturdily refused to be hurried. It came into being to meet the needs of man and his beasts, and it matched its pace to the pace of the beasts. Even in this age of mechanization and hurry it has, so far, managed to maintain its original function.

And it is this refusal to be hurried that has made the villages of England so beautiful. In these days of ever-increasing urbanization many people are inclined to think of the villages as pleasant picture-postcards, as "sweet," as rather "arty" (and maybe they are, if your standards are those of modern industrial architecture), but it is as well to remember that the "arty" never has a long life, being subject to the dictates of fashion, and that even works of art become museum pieces in the course of time. It is true that many villages are perfect examples of design and craftsmanship, but they certainly are not arty and they have never become museum pieces. They live, fulfilling the exact purpose for which they were originally constructed. That is true of many thousands of village buildings in England, of home and cottage, of barn and mill, of inn no less than church.

But it must not be thought that English villages were built to a pattern. To a shape, often—villages on the chalk tend to cluster around the church and the inn, or, if you look a little deeper into the matter, around the spring; villages in the flat grazing country tend to spread out, so that their ends are often out of sight of the church altogether, a shape that was dictated by the daily walking capacity of the cow from field to dairy just as the shape of the chalk village was dictated by the daily walking capacity of the woman from cottage to spring—but to pattern, never. There is no pattern. On the contrary, there is an absolutely unending variety in every village. But, also, there is always a general harmony. There is a wealth of detail, as the photographs in this book clearly show; but, as they also show, harmony has never been lost in the forest of detail because there has always been union between Nature and the handiwork of man.

## THE HUNT MOVES OFF, KERSEY

KERSEY, one of the most ancient of Suffolk villages, with its fine old Gothic church tower in the background as well as many sixteenth- and seventeenth-century houses, makes a most attractive setting for the start of a meet of the well-known Essex and Suffolk Hunt.

Very largely this has been maintained because man, until fairly recently, has always used the materials lying ready to his hand, the local stone and the local timber. It is because of this that there is a specific likeness in East Anglian villages, in the villages of the Weald, between certain Northamptonshire villages and villages on the Cotswolds, between the villages of the granite north and granite Cornwall. It is this that gives that essential "rightness" to English villages, so that they seem to grow out of the ground. It is not an effect that the builders consciously tried to obtain: it is the natural offspring of the union between man and Nature. In the same way, the old builders did not try to obtain a beautiful effect—it is probable that they never even thought about it—they merely used their common sense, and beauty followed. Building was always for a particular purpose, and always strictly utilitarian. But the old builders did the best job they could, because they were craftsmen and took an enormous pride in their work. Today it has become a commonplace to remark on the fitness of old rural buildings to their surroundings. In fact, there is nothing in the least remarkable about it, but the remark is a fitting commentary upon modern building and design, on the use of foreign materials in the place of local ones, on the decline in craftsmanship.

It is, I am afraid, beyond question that English village architecture is dead. I suppose that it would be true to say that, as a national force, it died many years ago. But the village lives. I have said that the important thing about the English village is its vitality. Never was this more clearly shown than in the years between the wars, when the village survived, though only just, the attack of modern education which taught the young countryman that the only jobs worth having were "white-collar" jobs and encouraged a mass migration to the towns. That attack was at least contained.

But it must be remembered that the conditions that gave to England the village organization proper are gone, probably, but not certainly, for ever. The conditions that gave birth to the genius which flowered in the best of English village architecture are gone, quite certainly, for ever. Yet still the village lives, is more alive in a way than ever before. Here is another example of this tremendous vitality, this astonishing resilience. Today there is the radio and the telephone and the grid system and omnibuses; the women's institute and the young farmers' club and the village hall and the travelling library. All these new things have been absorbed, but as much as possible of the old has been retained most doggedly —old customs and old ceremonials and the like. And even where they have not been retained in something approaching their original form, the dates of these old fairs and feasts are still marked by the appearance of coconut shies or dancing on the village green. It may be said with truth that the English village has risen to the occasion and grasped present opportunity. The old vitality is still there.

Yet, more than ever before, the future of the English village hangs in the

## AT AN OLD FORD OVER THE THAMES

MANY villages were founded at points where the rivers of southern England could be forded most easily. This view looking north from Streatley Hill shows the Thames at the point where it enters the chalk gorge, with Berkshire on the nearer bank and Oxfordshire on the farther one. Here there was a ford from the earliest times and a village on either side of it, Goring, seen on the right, and Streatley, which lies just behind the group of trees on the left. An early bridge was built across the river on the site of the ford, a bridge which used to be one of the most charming landmarks in this part of the Thames Valley. Like almost all the ancient Thames bridges it proved inadequate to carry the ever-increasing amount of week-end traffic, and the present concrete bridge, which was completed in 1923, now unites the two villages. These, like other Thames-side beauty-spots, are becoming increasingly popular with Londoners and attract large numbers of visitors each summer.

9

balance. It came into being as the best organization for the rural way of life. It is in that word "organization" that the fate of the village lies concealed. Is it still the best economic mode of organization for the times and the future? If it is not, then, though there will still be villages, village life will follow village architecture. Villages will become dormitories for town workers or homes of rest for those urban workers who have not been able to stand the pace. If in future the pace is everywhere to match the pace of the latest machine, then that will inevitably happen. There are many who maintain that that will be the course of events, many more who maintain that this present tendency to centralization must inevitably kill the village organization. I do not believe it.

On the contrary. I believe that with every extension of urbanization, with every increase in pace, the future of the English village becomes more assured as a place to live in. There are signs of that everywhere today. But there is also another and more hopeful sign. Villagers themselves are becoming conscious of their villages and their beauty, where once they took them for granted. They are taking pains to maintain them, partly, it must be admitted, for the benefit of tourists, but partly also for themselves, not only for the life without but also for the life within. There is still more than enough vitality in the village as an organization to ensure the future. The life so vividly pictured in this book will go on.

*Brian Vaughtsewald*

DUNTISBORNE ABBOTS, GLOUCESTERSHIRE, IN THE COTSWOLDS

## WIVENHOE ON THE COLNE

ON ITS way to the North Sea, which it enters at Mersea, the Essex Colne flows through Colchester, the county town, and five miles lower downstream reaches Wivenhoe, a village of which the attractive grouping is best appreciated when viewed from the farther bank of the river with which it is linked by ferry. The village was once an outrider of the Cinque Ports: it has retained its connexion with the sea and always has many yachts and pleasure-boats moored alongside its quay and in mid-stream. Yacht-building and yacht-repairing are among its present-day activities, whilst very occasionally a larger ship still goes into its yard for overhaul. Wivenhoe also is one of the traditional centres of the Essex oyster fisheries. Of the buildings themselves, the church, which is medieval, has been finely restored; many of the houses along the waterfront are in the most graceful Georgian style, and some others have examples of "pargeting," a form of relief-sculpture which is very common in Essex; in this instance a common feature of the designs is the cockle-shell.

# The South and East

THE English village which derives from the Anglo-Saxon prototype is most frequently found in the southern and south-eastern counties. That is inevitable because it was the South Country which was most intensively colonized by the Saxon settlers, who established thousands of communities by river and seashore in the period between the fall of Roman Britain and the conquest of Anglo-Saxon England by William of Normandy.

The typical Saxon settlement of the south consisted of the thane's house and the church, with a cluster of hovels around them, though often the church was at the north end of the village group. The thane's house became the manor or the manor-farm of the later Middle Ages, the church was often rebuilt again and again, and the cluster of wattle-and-daub hovels was transformed into the charming group of cottages which often distinguished Tudor and Elizabethan villages.

It is fanciful to suppose that modern villages—modern, that is, in the sense that they exist today—retain with any degree of exactness the plan of the Saxon original. It is by no means fanciful to say that hundreds of the villages of today are directly descended from the Anglo-Saxon settlements, with here and there a church which proclaims its Saxon origin, a manor-house which was undeniably a part of the fourteenth-century village, or a group of cottages built in the reign of Henry VII or Henry VIII.

To take a few examples at random from the wealth of interest which resides in the villages of the southern and south-eastern counties, Chiddingstone in Kent retains a whole row of cottages dating from the reign of Henry VII; its near neighbour, Penshurst, has a manor-house of which the great hall was built in the fourteenth century. Greensted, in Essex, can claim a church of which the nave is built from the trunks of oak trees dating at the latest from the tenth century. Aldbury, in Hertfordshire, has the stocks and whipping-posts by the village pond recalling medieval days when punishment was both summary and public. Worth, in Sussex, has a village church which is mainly Norman in masonry but retains exactly the ground plan of the Saxon church.

There are scores built around an eleventh- or twelfth-century church, such as Barfreston, in Kent, which possesses one of the loveliest of the tiny churches which the Normans so often built on the site of a Saxon chapel. Every second village in Kent and Sussex still shows at least one or two cottage homes of the sixteenth century. Several in the uplands of central Kent, such as Bredgar and Wormshill, are centred round a lovely manor-house which took shape in the heyday of the Kentish yeomen, while others, especially in Suffolk and northern Essex, retain the fine merchants' houses and the wool halls which are the outward signs of the prosperity these villages enjoyed when the late medieval wool boom was at its height. Hundreds of churches in those counties and in the wool country of Kent were rebuilt with tall towers and lofty naves in the late Gothic style of architecture current in the fifteenth century. Lavenham and Kersey in Suffolk, Finchingfield and Thaxted in Essex, belong to this tradition, though Finchingfield, in spite of its low, squat church tower, has a special place in any list of English villages by reason of its beautiful composition.

Much of the attraction of southern England's villages is due to the variety of building materials used during the many centuries in which the villages of today were taking shape. One misses the mellow colouring of the local stone used, for instance, in the Cotswold country, but there is something almost equally attractive in the stone belt of North Norfolk, where a number of seaside villages, including Stiffkey and Cley, are built almost throughout of the locally gathered cobblestones.

The rest of East Anglia is unusually poor in building stone, so that in the Middle Ages and later any material that came to hand was used. Many of the villages, therefore, are half-timbered because in the sixteenth and seventeenth centuries the whole of Essex and much of Suffolk was unusually well wooded with the remnants of the vast forest of Waltham which has now almost totally disappeared. Even the half-timbered style was too expensive for the bulk of rural cottages. In the country districts of Essex, Suffolk and Norfolk, lath and plaster, the descendant of the early style of wattle and daub, was the staple material of cottage architecture. The plaster covering of the cottages was often gaily colour-washed, and this local style gave rise to the most attractive facet of East Anglian village architecture, the parge work, or pargeting, consisting of designs worked on the plaster covering of cottages and houses. Many parge-work designs dating from the seventeenth century can still be seen, and many excellent though more modern imitations of it, which bring interest to many villages otherwise undistinguished.

In the downland country, and specially in the North Downs of Surrey and Kent, in the Chiltern Hills and in the South Downs of Sussex, there are many flint-built cottages and farmhouses. The material for these buildings is derived from the vast deposits of flint which occur in all the chalk country, the same flint from which prehistoric man who dwelt in these downlands made his implements.

Altogether there is unending variety not only in the style of individual villages or the materials from which their homes are built, but even in the many minor facets of village architecture. Many of these are entirely local, such as the thick thatched roofs of the Berkshire villages under the downs, the weatherboarding of the Kentish villages, the Horsham-stone roofs of the central marches of Sussex, and hanging tiles seen in villages near the boundaries of Surrey and Sussex.

## BRAY, BERKSHIRE

THE passage under the old house in the centre of the picture serves as the lichgate leading into the parish church seen in the background. Although the house over the passage has been largely rebuilt, some of its beams are over four hundred years old and there are records to show that this unusual form of approach to the church has been in use for more than five hundred years. Bray is a riverside village set close to the Thames and is one of the least commercialized of the Thames-side villages below Reading. Apart from its charm it has world-wide fame as the parish of the Rev. Simon Aleyn, reputed to have declared: "Whatsoever king doth reign, I will be the Vicar of Bray, sir." Simon Aleyn was as good as his word, for he was vicar in the reigns of Henry VIII, Edward VI, Mary and Elizabeth.

15

## ANCIENT VILLAGES OF KENT

LENHAM (*left*) and Eynsford (*below*) are both in their different ways characteristic of Kent's varied village architecture. The cobblestoned sidewalk which flanks one side of the square at Lenham, and is divided from it by the row of venerable trees seen in the picture, dates from the time—before the age of motor-cars—when Lenham was a flourishing place on the highroad between Maidstone and Ashford. A recent by-pass road has left it a quiet oasis just off the modern Dover road. The ford at Eynsford is over the River Darent. The stone bridge beside it dates from the fifteenth century. There was a Norman castle at Eynsford which helped to give the village early importance. Its well-built medieval houses show that it retained its importance for many centuries. One of the finest is the thatched and half-timbered Tudor house shown beyond the bridge.

## A ROADSIDE VILLAGE

THE church of Ightham is well away from the village proper at its north end, while the modern village straggles around a bend in the road which follows the line of the first main road from Maidstone to Sevenoaks. Thus the picture illustrates a very normal development of the village in the course of a thousand years. The original settlement, probably founded by the Saxons, was around the church. Through every change of fortune the church has retained its site, though several times rebuilt. Not so the village, which changed its position to conform with the growing importance of the roads in the sixteenth and seventeenth centuries, a period from which dates the half-timbered house in the centre of the picture facing on the "square." In very recent times the village has begun to grow away from its centre and lose the compactness which is the hall-mark of ancient places. Here, for instance, new bungalows and houses can be seen beside the main road at the right-hand upper edge of the photograph, illustrating an almost nation-wide development in Britain quite apart from the ribbon development along some arterial roads. The oast-houses (bottom, left) and the orchard between the village and the church represent the two characteristic rural activities of Kent, though within the last century the area under hops has decreased while the acreage of land devoted almost entirely to orchards shows a corresponding increase.

## CHIDDINGSTONE VILLAGE

THE picturesque quality of Chiddingstone village, situated in the Weald of Kent between Edenbridge and Tonbridge, has captured the imagination of many artists and poets. It is apparent in this photograph, looking down the village street, with the wall of the churchyard and lichgate on the right and the ancient row of cottages framed by the mellow trees of the churchyard. Chiddingstone is the village of the Streatfielde family, who have been associated with it since 1500, an even longer time than the Sidneys with Penshurst or the Sackvilles with Knole. There is a gravestone in the parish church which bears a memorial: "To Richard Streatfielde who died in 1601." He is described as being "greene in years but ripe in faith and fruites." The epitaph ends: "God hath his soul, this towne his fame, the poor a portion large of all his worldly store." Thus are commemorated the good works of an Elizabethan gentleman whose rebuilding of the village to house the dependants of the manor is a still eloquent memorial of his fame. He was the last of a line of lords of the manor who took part in the building of this model village, for in the long row of cottages shown here almost all date from his time or earlier. The name Chiddingstone is often thought to be a corruption of "chiding stone"; a large rock is held by some to be a judgment stone used by the Druids. The stone was not imported, but is part of the natural rock formation which has resisted erosion, as have a number of detached rocks near Tunbridge Wells.

## A MEDIEVAL VILLAGE

This view of Aylesford, one of the most picturesque Kent villages, shows the ancient bridge which spans the Medway, and the row of attractive houses which builds up to the high-set medieval church. Aylesford's story starts in Roman times, when there was a ford across the river much used by traffic from the chain of Roman towns spread along Watling Street between Rochester and London. This crossing of the Medway was important in the Middle Ages; ultimately what was then an exceptionally fine bridge was built at the end of the fifteenth century, replacing an earlier one then about two hundred years old. The present bridge remains substantially the same as that early Tudor structure and it is one of the most ancient in southern England. The central wide-span archway, made necessary to facilitate navigation, replaced two narrow spans of the medieval bridge; but otherwise it has been little altered and, by modern standards, the roadway it carries is very narrow. The original church was Norman, and was rebuilt in the fifteenth century, but the lower part of the tower as it stands today is part of the original Norman fabric. An unfounded tradition has it that this tower was originally part of a castle. Yet another link connects Aylesford with the Middle Ages, for a medieval religious house, dating back to 1240 and recently refounded, was established here as a brotherhood of Carmelite friars and is still called the Friary. Originally it was a monastery of a mendicant order.

## ON A CREEK OF CHICHESTER HARBOUR

THIS aerial view of Bosham shows the features of the village which make it one of the most distinctive in southern England. The creek on which it lies, and which has determined its long and eventful history, is filled now with sailing craft and pleasure-boats, but was formerly the "highway" of many fishing craft which were the basis of Bosham's prosperity. The creeks of Chichester harbour, like the eastern estuaries of Essex, were used again and again by invaders in ancient times, when there came to Sussex in turn Romans, Saxons and Vikings. There is a tradition that raiding Vikings carried away the bells of Bosham Church, but they foundered in the creek; it is said that the bells can still be heard sometimes in stormy weather sounding as an echo of the ones in use today.

# FEUDAL VILLAGE

PENSHURST still represents the feudal England of tradition and many parts of the village remain as they were five hundred years ago. The manor-house, the famous Penshurst Place, stands at the village end of its beautiful timbered park. Close by, the church is set between the manor and the village proper, which is centred on the meeting place of the three roads which radiate from the village. Penshurst is the home of the Sidney family. The present owner, Lord De L'Isle and Dudley, is a Sidney. The illustrious Sir Philip Sidney was born in Penshurst Place in 1554. The first Sidney to live here was Sir William Sidney, to whom the manor was given by Edward VI. Prior to that Penshurst was in the possession of the Dukes of Buckingham and in Norman times of the Penchesters, of which Penshurst is a corruption. The irregularly shaped Place is the work of many centuries, but the core of the old manor-house remains in the Great Hall, built in the fourteenth century.

## ALFRISTON, SUSSEX

ALFRISTON is a large village in the valley of the Cuckmere which here runs between two ridges of the South Downs. Its interest lies partly in its old buildings and partly in its traditional associations. Among the many ancient houses in its long main street, the Star Inn, shown in this picture, is notable. The fine timber beams of the façade are said to date from 1500. Though the records are incomplete it seems certain that the building is a genuine Tudor one. The unique carvings in wood which embellish the exterior are another feature of great interest. Alfriston's associations derive from its position near the mouth of the little Cuckmere river. Before the organization of the coastguard service smuggling was most profitable and Alfriston was one of the centres from which smugglers operated.

## SUSSEX BANK HOLIDAY

SOUTH HARTING is the scene of this animated cameo of village life as the local band marches through the village street on a Bank Holiday morning, passing the booths of the village fair and followed by most of the child population and a good many of their elders, too. South Harting is one of scores of villages which nestle under the northern slopes of the Sussex downs whose blurred outline can be seen in the background. It is one of the largest of these villages whose whole life has always been linked with the varying fortunes of Sussex agriculture. Originally they were settlements founded by the Saxons well above the tangled undergrowth and swampy marshes of the Weald, yet low enough to take advantage of the richer soil where the chalk of the downs gives way to the clay of the valleys. In the later Middle Ages South Harting, like its neighbours, grew wealthy from making the best of both worlds—from the sheep-walks of the downs when the woollen trade was prosperous and from the corn crops of the lowlands when arable farming was more profitable. There is a still-present sign of this in the fine church which is exceptionally large for the size of the village. Its graceful spire caps a thirteenth-century building of which the Early English triple lancets in the east wall are visible. Anthony Trollope, the famous Victorian novelist, whose reputation became established with the publication of *Barchester Towers*, lived in South Harting for many years and ultimately was buried there.

## LOWLAND VILLAGES OF SUSSEX

THE South Downs of Sussex have always been so celebrated by poet and traveller alike that the beauties of the Weald and the river valleys are often overlooked. Wisborough Green (*above*) is one of many similar and delightful villages in the Weald, the hanging tiles and weatherboarding of its cottages are distinctively Sussex and most of its cottage homes face on to the broad green. Piddinghoe (*below*) is one of the villages in the Ouse Valley between Lewes and Newhaven. The round tower of its church, like those of South-ease and Lewes itself, may have been used as a beacon tower to guide mariners navigating the estuary of the Ouse. They are the only three round towers in Sussex. The weather-vane visible on top of the spire is the "begilded dolphin" remembered by Rudyard Kipling, who wrote so many poems on the countryside: "Where Piddinghoe's begilded dolphin veers."

## POYNINGS AND THE DYKE HILLS

THE long ridge of the South Downs from the Dyke Hills on the extreme left to Chancton-bury Ring, which is just off the right of the picture, forms the backcloth against which the village of Poynings is etched in detail. The farm buildings and cottages are grouped around the cruciform medieval church distinctive for its squat, square tower. Other smaller farms and cottages are half hidden in the generous woodlands which thrive on the lower ground in contrast with the bare grassy ridges of the downs. The name Poynings is as much a part of Sussex history as the village is of its rural beauty, for the Poynings family, from early medieval times onward, were lords of the manor famous for their good deeds at home and their bravery in war. One of the most famous of the line was Michael, Baron Poynings, a hero of the battles of Crécy and Poitiers, to whom is due the rebuilding of the present church, which is thus a link with one of the most illustrious periods of British history. The sharp and clearly defined contrast in Sussex rural life between the sheep-walks of the downs and the mixed farming of the lowlands is here perfectly illustrated.

## SURREY BEAUTY-SPOT

THIS is a part of the village of Shere overlooked by many visitors who see only the cottages and houses on the main road from Guildford to Dorking. Shere lies in the valley of the Tillingbourne, a little river which separates the chalk country of the Surrey Downs from the sandstone country, the heather-covered commons and pine woods rising on the south toward Winterfold Heath and Windmill Hill. It is one of the many Surrey villages founded by the Saxons on the fringe of the great Forest of Anderida, which covered most of Surrey south of the downland ridge. Its life has been devoted for more than a thousand years to working the comparatively fertile land on either bank of the Tillingbourne, where there are still lush meadows close to the river and a strip of ploughed land before the grassy slopes of the downs are reached on the one hand and the heaths of the sandstone hills on the other. Many of Shere's village homes date from the days of the Tudor and Stuart kings. The church is of particular interest. There are traces of pre-Norman work in its fabric and definite evidence of a Norman church of approximately the same size and shape as the present one, which was rebuilt in the thirteenth century. Then, apart from an enlargement of the whole fabric, the upper storey (clearly seen in the photograph) was added to the low Norman tower and, probably at the same time, the handsome octagonal timber spire.

# ANCIENT TOWN, MODERN VILLAGE

THE mellow beauty of these ancient cottages in Bletchingley, Surrey, has all the charm of old-world village architecture. Yet Bletchingley was once a borough, a market town of considerable importance, which included Lord Palmerston among many distinguished members which it returned to Parliament. Considering that Bletchingley is no more than three miles from Redhill, Surrey's most modern and most rapidly enlarging town, it is amazing how relatively unspoilt it has remained and how successfully secluded corners like this have defied the modern builder to displace them. Among the famous families who have held the castle and the manor of Bletchingley are the Clares, the Staffords and the Howards of Effingham, all wealthy families, as well as famous families who kept the cottages and houses of the town in constantly good repair. That is the reason why so many fine old buildings like those pictured here have been bequeathed to the present. Notice the contrast between the bare timber-framed construction and the decorative hanging tiles of the upper storey in the foreground building, a theme repeated farther along the row with unusually picturesque effect. The "hanging tile" technique is one of several methods used from Tudor times onward to ensure that the village buildings should be watertight— a very necessary protection before the era of building in brick or concrete had begun, except in the Cotswold country and other areas where stone has been used for cottage building from time immemorial. Different means of protection against the weather became associated with different parts of the countryside. In South-east England, for instance, hanging tiles were most frequently used in Surrey and Sussex, while the simpler weather-boarding is found most often in Kent. Whatever the material, the underlying principle is the same—rain flows down the facing, each layer of which overlaps the one below, while the bottom storey is generally protected from the weather by the overhang of the upper one.

## OLD GODSTONE

GODSTONE, though only just over twenty miles from London, is another village almost entirely neglected by twentieth-century "progress," partly because it is more than two miles from the nearest railway station. It lies just under the Surrey downs where they are crossed by the main road from London to Eastbourne. Part of the village well known to travellers along this road is pleasantly grouped round a green, though the church and the other buildings pictured here are a full half-mile away, connected with the green by a metalled footpath. The church (spire visible in the background) is a nineteenth-century restoration of a medieval building. The graceful buildings are a part of the St. Mary's Almshouses, not a medieval group, but successful copies of the Tudor style.

## HOLMBURY ST. MARY

HOLMBURY ST. MARY, like Peaslake (*opposite*), is one of the several villages in the deep valleys between the upstanding hills of the greensand ridge, which is part of the long range of hills parallel with the North Downs and extending from the Hindhead countryside in the west to the Kentish hills near Sevenoaks in the east. This photograph from the slopes of Holmbury Hill is looking across the valley to the dense pinewoods which rise toward the summit of Leith Hill, the highest point in the range. During the Second World War this wooded area was a site on which large quantities of ammunition were stacked, for the thick woods gave good concealment and the thinly populated country enabled the ammunition stacks to be spaced out safely over a wide area through which ran good roads that made access easy.

28

## VILLAGE OF THE HURT WOOD

SURREY's Hurt Wood includes some of the most spectacular scenery in the whole of the Home Counties. The woodlands cover thousands of acres of hill country, while toward the valley of the Tillingbourne they are broken by narrow strips of more fertile lowland in which there are small villages. Peaslake, seen here from one of the twin ridges which hem it in closely, is set in one of these valleys at the extreme northern end of the pinewood country. An ancient hamlet rather than a village, it has grown considerably within the memory of the oldest inhabitants, and has little intrinsic beauty of village architecture. It still makes a charming picture from this view-point with its few old cottages half hidden by the trees which come down almost to the valley floor. In the left background by the modern chapel and village cemetery is one of the many long tracks which radiate from Peaslake and lead uphill for more than two miles along the ridge to the 900-ft. summit of the plateau. This track leads to and ends at one of the highest view-points of the range, Coneyhurst Hill. Although the characteristic tree of the Hurt Wood is the pine, the photograph shows how on the lower ground, where the hard sandstone subsoil has a thin covering of clay, the evergreens are interspersed with deciduous English forest trees.

## CHURCHES AND COTTAGES OF ESSEX

ESSEX villages, even those comparatively near London, are specially favoured in the beauty of their cottage architecture and the varied nature of their ancient churches. This is due in no small measure to the fact that Essex has been a thriving agricultural county since the later Middle Ages and, except for restricted areas such as that along the estuary of the Thames, has escaped industrial development on a major scale. The village has retained surprisingly the real unity of county life. Cottages originally well built have lasted far beyond their normal span. Many more than four hundred years old are still inhabited and in a state of good repair. With no call to build new churches to cater for greatly increased parishes, the old churches of the county have also survived more or less intact. On these pages are shown two of the most characteristic of Essex village churches, representing the earliest and the latest periods of medieval building, as well as cottages dating from the sixteenth and seventeenth centuries in the two contrasting styles of Essex buildings. The church of Greensted-juxta-Ongar (*top, left*) is a justly famous building because it is one of the very few churches left in Britain in which the handiwork of the Saxon builders is plainly seen. In this case the photograph shows well one wall of the nave which is composed of the trunks of oak trees split in half. Most Saxon churches, certainly those earlier than the eleventh

30

century, were of timber, but this is the only one in the world to retain its original timber nave. The oak has had to be repaired, and in one or two instances replaced, but a number of the "beams" are in a remarkable state of preservation and likely to last for hundreds of years to come. The cottages at Hatfield Broad Oak (*bottom, left*) were built in the sixteenth century and show no sign of ceasing to be useful, though the thatched roof, of course, needs constant attention and periodic replacement. Cromwellian cottages are very common in Essex and neighbouring Hertfordshire, but earlier ones such as these are comparatively rare in any part of Britain. Notice the gay whitewash covering. Essex cottages themselves are sometimes of timber framing, at other times lath and plaster (or "wattle and daub" as it used to be called). Thaxted Church (*top, right*) is one of the earliest medieval churches in Essex, a fine example of the Perpendicular style of Gothic, rebuilt at a time when the woollen boom was at its height. Dancing along the church path are members of the local folk-dancing society which, since 1910, has revived with great success a pastime which was once an important part of village life. High Ongar (*bottom, right*), a tiny village on the road from Chipping Ongar to Chelmsford, shows in this quaint corner a half-timbered house in a style well known in the West Country but seldom seen in Essex homes. Here, too, a whitewash covering lightens the building and throws the fine timber beams into sharp relief.

31

# OLD ESSEX

FINCHINGFIELD, in the little-known countryside of northern Essex, is the scene of this charming photograph which is taken looking across a little stream to a row of ancient cottages building up gracefully to the squat church tower. The old mill in the background is no longer used for grinding corn, but serves as a still-present link with the time when the miller was one of the most prosperous of all the men residing in the neighbourhood.

## HEYBRIDGE MILL, BLACKWATER RIVER

THE old mills along the banks of many Essex rivers are a picturesque survival from the time when every village in the corn-growing country had its own mill. A large trade between the estuary mills and the London docks is still done by coastal vessels, some of them sailing barges. At one time the Blackwater and Colne estuaries were the haunts of smugglers and there is little doubt that many of the old mills which still line the waterways in these parts were extensively used for the hiding of contraband goods until such time as it was felt safe to remove them—often by road. Mills and millhouses can make attractive village groups in themselves, as here at Heybridge on the Blackwater near Maldon, where the Georgian millhouse and well-equipped mill appear in a dazzling coat of whitewash.

## IN RURAL NORFOLK

NORFOLK remains especially rich in small but ancient market towns which have maintained themselves but never expanded and are now no larger than many villages. Wymondham (*left*) is one of these. The market cross, framing the main street of the little town, was built at the beginning of the seventeenth century on the site of a much earlier one and retains almost exactly its original appearance. The old market hall of New Buckenham (*below*), a fine timber-and-plaster structure, has space beneath for the covered market. The tower of the parish church is a good example of the late Gothic style of architecture.

## NORFOLK BY THE SEA

MANY medieval ports and fishing villages of Norfolk have suffered greatly from the sea. In places it has receded and left former ports high and dry. In others encroachment has swept away towns. Blakeney (*right*), now a quiet village on the north coast, was once a port with an important coastwise trade. The sea has receded, leaving a wide stretch of salt-marsh, now a wildfowl sanctuary, whilst a creek flowing to the old quay holds barely sufficient water for the anchorage of even small fishing boats. Sea Palling (*below*) is another ancient settlement; here sand-dunes already have reached the edge of the village.

## IN THE NORWICH COUNTRYSIDE

NORWICH has always been the true hub of East Anglian rural life as well as its administrative and social centre. Within a fifteen-mile radius of the city it is possible to see from one village the tower or spire of the next parish church. This is especially true of the corn-growing country in the triangle bounded by Wymondham, Norwich and Bungay. Mulbarton, pictured here, takes added charm from its position on the common-like green.

## THE OLD BAILEY, CASTLE ACRE

THE gateway of this medieval castle marks the approach to the village of Castle Acre in Norfolk. The main street seen through the gateway is named Bailey Street, after the bailey of the castle. The castle itself was built by William de Warrenne in early Norman days. The village gateway dates from a rebuilding and extension of the castle about a hundred years later. Little else now remains of the once great fortress. Much of the material from which it was built was used in the construction of the village.

## ON THE EDGE OF BROADLAND

MANY Broadland villages have grown apace since the increased popularity of yachting as a pastime and holiday activity. A few of them, however, especially those away from the main yachting centres, are still beautiful and sequestered. Woodbastwick (*below*) is one of the most charming. The thatched village pump stands on a triangular green, while the old cottages and the fine Gothic church are half hidden by the mature trees, which are a feature of all the Broadland country except in the marshland which surrounds the Broads rivers where they approach the sea in the hinterland of Yarmouth and Lowestoft. Woodbastwick is set on a low ridge of higher ground which has been well cultivated since the time of the Anglian settlements, in contrast with the level plain, much of which was impenetrable swamp until the present lush Broadland pastures were reclaimed by scientific draining of the land enthusiastically fostered by local authorities in many other counties.

## THREE HISTORIC VILLAGES

CAVENDISH (*above*), Lavenham (*below, left*), and Monks Eleigh (*below, right*) are representative of the many handsome villages and small towns in that part of Suffolk which lies between Bury St. Edmunds and the valley of the Stour. This countryside benefited perhaps more than any other from the prosperity of the woollen trade in the fourteenth and fifteenth centuries. The wealth of the woollen merchants helped to swell the funds for rebuilding the village churches. Notice the stair turret at one corner of Cavendish's handsome tower, also

## OF THE SUFFOLK COUNTRYSIDE

the many thatched cottages along the green, several of them nearly four hundred years old. The Dukes of Devonshire take their family name from this village. The fine timber-framed houses in Lavenham, one with a plaster upper storey, were originally the homes of the merchants who dealt in wool. The cottage homes of Monks Eleigh, though on a much more modest scale, are all of about the same date and illustrate the link which exists between these three villages and many of the other villages and small towns of this farming district.

## OLD-WORLD VILLAGES IN LONDON'S COUNTRY

MUCH HADHAM (*top, left*), Aldbury (*bottom, left*), Little Missenden (*top, right*) and Chenies (*bottom, right*) are all distinguished villages of the countryside, yet none of them is more than thirty-five miles from London. In the variety of their cottage styles and in their characteristic grouping they represent the no mean beauty of Hertfordshire and Buckinghamshire villages. These counties, like Essex, have largely defied modern industry. The villages of Hertfordshire have always been prosperous because of the wealth of the land and have adapted themselves to the changing conditions of agriculture. Even when rural re-housing has added a modern "suburb," the core of the old village remains. Though Greater London has spread into the foothills of the Chilterns, there are still a number of unspoilt villages in Buckinghamshire, most of them smaller than those of neighbouring Hertfordshire because of the comparative poverty of the Chiltern soil. Much Hadham is a village strung out along the road, in contrast with Aldbury, which is grouped closely about the church. The plaster-covered and thatched cottages in Much Hadham, side by side with the half-timbered and weatherboarded houses, illustrate the two most common styles of Hertfordshire village homes, the half-timbered style being usually reserved for the larger and wealthier houses. Thus at Aldbury, where the stocks and whipping-post are in the foreground, the old manor-house behind is an exceptionally well restored, half-timbered house of the Tudor period. In both Little Missenden and Chenies the half-timbered building style of the traditional Buckinghamshire village is evident.

## CRAFTS AND CRAFTSMEN OF THE SOUTH AND EAST

READING from left to right across the top of these pages we show a thatcher at work in Surrey; parchment makers in Hampshire treating sheep pelts in the lime pits, a process that takes from five to six weeks; an Essex blacksmith shoeing farm greys; coopers at work in Rother-hithe—here oak staves from old pipes, hogsheads, octaves and puncheons are being dressed on a "horse" for conversion into smaller barrels. On the left is a cobbler of Blakeney, in Norfolk; on the right a furniture-maker at Hatfield Peverel, in Essex, is wax-polishing an oak refectory table made in the Jacobean style. Reading from left to right across the bottom of the pages we show a potter at work in Cook-ham, Berkshire; a craftsman at Chichester, in Sussex, "bearning" the hide of a sheep,

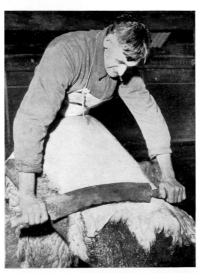

that is, removing the fatty tissue by means of a special curved knife; a cricket ball is being stitched by a craftsman at Teston, near Maidstone, in Kent; finishing off a cricket bat by planing the back of the blade to shape in a workshop in Surrey; saplings gathered from the woodlands on the borders of Surrey and Sussex are here being made into walking sticks; last, but not least, is a basket-maker at Alton, Hampshire. These and other handicrafts are still widely practised in the country-side, and though the genius of this mechanical age can mass-produce some of the things so made—such as boots and china-ware—for many of the others the machine is as yet no complete substitute for the real craftsman, though, as for example in the making of cricket bats, much initial rough work is now sometimes done by some form of machine, the crafts-man supplying only finishing touches.

## IN THE NEW FOREST

MOST of the New Forest villages are small and rather scattered clearings in the woodlands. Here and there, however, as in this hamlet near Lyndhurst (*above*), there are groups of beautiful thatched or stone-built cottages which take added distinction from their position facing the "lawns" which break up the forest woodlands. Beaulieu (*below*) is a large and picturesque village at the head of one of the creeks of Southampton Water. Here was founded a great Cistercian abbey at the beginning of the thirteenth century; the parish church of modern Beaulieu was originally the monks' refectory. One of the abbey buildings became the seat of the Montagu family and is still used as a residence. A little stream flowing down from the high ground of the New Forest widens just before it enters the tidal creek into the broad reed-fringed lake shown below. The many picturesque and ancient houses backing on to the lake-side are the first view of Beaulieu which is seen by visitors approaching from the direction of Lyndhurst and on the somewhat narrower highway from Hythe.

## GODSHILL, ISLE OF WIGHT

THE Isle of Wight has been well named England's "Garden Isle." With a small area, the circumference of which is less than seventy miles, it includes several of the most distinguished types of English scenery—a long ridge of chalk downs, a coast which varies from the abrupt chines of the south to the sandy beaches of the north, and a number of small towns and villages which, away from the coast, retain the charm and distinction of the finest south-country villages. Godshill, pictured here, is one of the oldest and most picturesque. The church, which is large by comparison with the size of the village, stands on a low hill and is flanked by a group of thatched cottages, whose steep roofs and tiny windows breaking the line of the thatch proclaim their ancient origin, which was probably in the sixteenth century. Godshill lies under the northern face of the downs on the main road between Newport and Ventnor, and commands from its modest eminence an unusually fine view over the central valley of the island towards Arreton Down and the ridge which links the east coast with the valley of the Medina, which is situated to the south of Newport.

## THE TICHBORNE DOLE

ENGLISH village life strikes many country people as dull or stereotyped, especially in these days when many links which bound the villagers with the lord of the manor have been severed. Most Saxon villages originated as family settlements, being extended to include collateral branches and only gradually embracing unrelated groups. The feudal system grew from this Saxon unit. By the time of the later Norman kings, though the village group had widened so far as its heredity was concerned, its members were related by ties of necessity and loyalty to its lord—the lower orders becoming automatically the lord's servants and supporters. This reciprocal loyalty maintained the essential unity of the parish through the latter part of the Middle Ages, even when the feudal system was only a memory. All that now survives of this link is tradition. The legal ties have long since ended and the powers of the lord of the manor have been transferred to established central and local authorities. Many old customs, some dating back to the Middle Ages, survive, however, including a number of doles instituted by the lord of the manor and retained by fortuitous circumstances. The Biddenden Dole in Kent is a notable one; the Tichborne Dole of Hampshire (*above*) another. Legend relates that the gifts of flour which are distributed from Tichborne House (near Alresford in Hampshire) were instituted eight hundred years ago, a former Lady Tichborne having laid a curse on the family if they failed to make the dole. Only one year has passed without the distribution being made.

# VILLAGE WITHIN A TEMPLE

THIS dramatic aerial view shows the village of Avebury, the whole of which, apart from the church and the manor-house, lies within the circle of a great prehistoric temple. The photograph also clearly shows on the left a number of the standing stones which are the remains of a complex of stone circles erected within the encircling trench and bank. Avebury was probably a temple of sun-worship a little earlier than Stonehenge and constructed by Stone Age man about four thousand years ago. There is no evidence that the site was occupied after the beginning of the Christian era until the Saxons founded a village on the site which is now occupied by the church and manor-house. Medieval roads were driven north–south and east–west through the earthworks so that when the village began to spread it grew up round the crossroad in the centre of the circle instead of round the church. Some of the stones from the original circles were used to surface the roads in the Middle Ages. Others were broken up and probably contributed materials to the building of some of the houses and cottages which were erected in the neighbourhood in the Middle Ages.

## LACOCK—MEDIEVAL VILLAGE

LACOCK in Wiltshire, which has retained an atmosphere of the Middle Ages, is a village of outstanding interest and varied history. The old buildings now vested in the National Trust are preserved as a living monument to the grace and beauty of English village architecture in the same way as many villages in other counties. The photograph gives a fine impression of stone building and half-timber work and the steep-pitched gables which make the village so distinctive. The building on the right is nearly six hundred years old. Other cottages and larger houses shown are at least four hundred years old and well preserved. Much of Lacock's medieval fame arose from its proximity to a nunnery, founded in 1232, of which Ela, Countess of Salisbury, was the first abbess. The Countess was one of the most pious women of her time. She had the distinction of laying the foundation stone of Salisbury Cathedral, and her ideals, perpetuated in Lacock Abbey, persisted for centuries after her death. Even at the time of the dissolution the conduct and piety of the nuns was highly praised by the commission set up by Henry VIII to examine the monastic foundations. Lacock Abbey was dissolved in 1539, part of its fabric being later built into a mansion.

## CASTLE COMBE

WILTSHIRE has an unusual number of villages which combine picturesque qualities with strong historic interest. On both these counts Castle Combe provokes comparison with Lacock (*opposite*). It lies in a hollow of the downs near Chippenham—the combe which gives it its name. The other part of its title recalls the cause of its medieval importance, for, whereas the traditions of Lacock were religious, those of Castle Combe were, from the earliest times until the Middle Ages, military. These two villages reflect the most important facets of life in England between the Saxon settlements and the beginning of Tudor times. Castle Combe may have originated as a prehistoric fortress village—for there was once a Saxon fortress of timber within its earthworks. This was succeeded by a Norman castle of stone, which, in spite of early fame, quickly fell into disrepair until today practically nothing is left of it. Castle Combe developed into a market town during the later Middle Ages. Its market cross, from which this photograph, looking down the village street, is taken, unlike the market cross at Wymondham in Norfolk (see page 34), is a square stone pedestal approached by two steps with a pier supporting a timber roof.

49

## WINDMILLS

WINDMILLS were in use before the twelfth century, first becoming common in Germany and the Low Countries. Early windmills were of two distinct types: the German, or post mill, the body of which revolved on a central post so that the mill sails could be trimmed to the wind, and the Dutch mill, called also tower, smock or frock mill, in which the main building remained stationary while the top part revolved and the mill shaft with its bearings turned with it. The method of working the mill was the same for both types of building. The sails, of which there might be four, five or six, though normally four only, consisted of canvas stretched over crossed wooden slats. The canvas could be furled like the sails of a ship for safety in high winds. The first mills were turned to the wind by hand, but later a small wheel or fantail was fitted to the back of the mill and this caused the wind itself to turn the mill. Reading down from the top left-hand corner, and finishing with the photograph at the top right-hand corner, the pictures show a close

view of the fantail mechanism of Terling Mill, in Essex; the mill at Upminster, in Essex; the post mill at Stansfield, Suffolk, which has an unusual gallery round the top; the mill at Mountnessing, Essex; the mill at Saltfleet, Lincolnshire; tower mill at Pakenham, Suffolk; post mill at Brill, Buckinghamshire, and the mill at Rye, in Sussex. Though windmills are no longer in general use for grinding corn, they are often employed in rural districts both for pumping water and to help in the charging of electric batteries.

SEATOLLER, CUMBERLAND

# Northern England

GREY wind-swept moors, a rugged and often inhospitable coastline, supreme beauty of line rather than of colour—those are the main features of the picture which the Pennine country and the moorlands and coast of Northumberland offer to the traveller. Every northerner, of course, will swear that there is much more to it than that, every southerner who has grown to know and love the northern moors will agree whole-heartedly. None will deny that the austerity, even the greyness, of the scene is reflected in the villages of the north, many of which are built of the local stone and thus partake of the dominant colour scheme of the countryside in general.

What a difference there is between the grey stone-built villages in the high valleys of the Pennines and the grey stone-built villages of the Cotswold country. In sober fact it is the difference in the colour of the stone (even though both are tones of grey) which creates the wide gulf between the two. The beauty of northern villages is akin to the beauty of the grand yet sometimes forbidding scenery in which they are set.

Villages are far fewer than in the south, for the north country has never supported a rural population half as dense as that which lives on the land of the southern counties. There are hundreds of square miles of the Pennine country without a village in sight. The villages, with few exceptions, are confined to the long valleys which wind down through the hills towards the Vale of York and the coastal plain of Northumberland and the short, steep valleys which fall away on the west towards the coastal plain of Lancashire and Cheshire.

In these valleys, in Wharfedale, in Nidderdale, in the Trough of Bowland, and in the Pennine valleys of Durham and Northumberland, there are many villages which fit admirably into their own special setting and have a very real beauty and interest. Among them Pateley Bridge, Kettlewell and Ramsgill are particularly lovely and beautifully composed. Bolton Abbey is one of the loveliest beauty-spots in the north, but the near-by village is a little disappointing.

The Vale of York itself is rich agricultural country, more densely peopled than most of the rural North. Its villages are correspondingly more numerous and in many ways akin to their southern counterparts, compactly built round the church and manor-farm with perhaps an old mill or a few well-built sixteenth-century cottages to remind us of their early prosperity.

The fortress villages of the Northumberland coast are utterly fascinating. Some of them, like Bamburgh (if Bamburgh can rightly be called a village), are entirely dominated by their castle, as completely as Corfe Castle in Dorset dominates the village below it. Very different are the few fishing villages which lie along the coast of the North Riding of Yorkshire, where the North York Moors end in a glorious riot of cliff scenery, and villages such as Staithes and Robin Hood's Bay have much of the quality of their counterparts along the coast of Devon and Cornwall. The making of jet ornaments and the gathering of the raw material have brought to Whitby and its neighbouring villages a rare prosperity quite independent of the varying fortunes of the fishing industry.

The villages of Derbyshire deserve more than a passing thought. They have much in common with those of the Yorkshire dales, for the vigour of the two landscapes is based on the same qualities, and the stone of which the villages are built is similar in both areas. The Pennine Hills south of the Peak break up into a series of limestone gorges, of which Dovedale is the most famous, though in scenery and character almost identical with half a dozen others less well known. Milldale and Tissington and Ilam stand out, though there may be others which the connoisseur of village architecture would choose in preference. They are all mainly stone-built villages merging into the prevailing colours of the limestone landscape like the Pennine villages of Yorkshire and Lancashire. They are all well built with a few fine and graceful houses and some lovely old churches. Tissington has a special place among English villages because of the traditional well-dressing ceremony associated with it, and because of the beauty of the architecture of its Norman church.

The villages of the Lake District are far more colourful with a tradition of gay gardens, a riot of multi-coloured flowers. Another tradition enlivens the village scene, that of the gay colourwash which decorates many a cottage and more elaborate house. The impression which most of the villages in the deep valleys give is one of brightness and beauty admirably set off by the grandeur of the scenery, with nearly always a high peak in the background and perhaps a lake forming part of Nature's wide canvas on which the village is, as it were, painted.

Cheshire is a genuine part of the North Country, but its landscapes and its villages are utterly different from anything else in the northern half of England. The villages have their own character and their own traditions which owe nothing to any other part of the country. In the main Cheshire is a lowland county, once densely afforested. In that respect only it shares the tradition of the other Marcher counties in that its stone-built villages are few, its half-timbered buildings numerous and beautiful. Sandbach is famous because of its two Celtic crosses. For the most part the villages are quiet centres of an intensively cultivated countryside, distinguished by the black and white of half-timbered houses and cottages and the elaborate magpie designs which decorate the façades of many buildings great and small.

## MILLDALE, STAFFORDSHIRE

THE River Dove divides Staffordshire from Derbyshire for much of its course, so that the western side of Dovedale is in Staffordshire, the eastern side in Derbyshire. Here the Pennine Chain enters its last phase and breaks into a number of limestone gorges, of which Dovedale is the longest and most impressive. A number of villages lie in the valley, though above Ashbourne it is nowhere broad enough for the growth of any considerable town. Milldale, pictured above, is on the Staffordshire bank; its beauty, like so many of the moorland villages of the north, derives from its position rather than from the architecture of its cottages or any other special feature. Here the cliff-like hills which hem in the Dove recede and allow a motor road to come down from the uplands into the heart of the valley. The village cottages are stone-built and grey without the warmth of the stone-built cottages of the Cotswold country; but there is warmth in the hearts of the hard-working rural people who make their living by tending the sheep and cattle which range over the pastures,

## IN OLD HAWKSHEAD

HAWKSHEAD is one of the largest of Lake District villages. Though the scenery around is similar to that of Cumberland and Westmorland, Hawkshead is in fact in that part of Lancashire known as the Furness Peninsula. William Wordsworth, poet of the Lake District, was educated here at the Grammar School. The church, a very late medieval building, is on high ground away from the village and commands, as the photograph below shows, a magnificent view over the valley to the Lakeland fells, dimly seen in the background. The left-hand photograph shows some of Hawkshead's many old houses which have overhanging upper storeys.

## ANCIENT VILLAGE CROSSES IN SANDBACH

IN THE early days of Christianity a large number of crosses were set up in villages and at crossroads in the north and west. Celtic in origin, they often preceded the establishment of a church and were regarded as most sacred symbols. Two of these crosses, which have been beautifully carved, have been re-erected in the market place of Sandbach, Cheshire.

## VILLAGES OF NORTHUMBERLAND

BAMBURGH (*below*), situated in the far north of the county, was the capital of a small Saxon kingdom before England had any semblance of unity. According to tradition it takes its name from a Saxon queen, Bebbe, who lived in the sixth century. A Saxon castle was built here on a great outcrop of basalt rock, and the Norman castle, of which the square keep can be seen on the left of the photograph, was erected on the same site. This castle served as a fortress palace until the Civil War. Raids and forays were frequent in the Border country, so the village, mainly stone-built, grew up clustering literally in the shadow of the castle. Wallbottle (*above*), also stone-built but less compact and less ancient than Bamburgh, grew up in an area far less subject to armed conflict. It is five miles to the west of Newcastle-on-Tyne in countryside where today agriculture and coal-mining exist side by side.

## WATENDLATH

THE hamlet of Watendlath at the head of the tarn of that name in Cumberland is three miles to the south of Keswick. Watendlath Vale, in which it lies, is traversed by a stream called the Lodore and is separated by a low ridge from Borrowdale. In the left background can be seen Great Gable. In contrast with the tree-clad slopes of Dovedale (see page 61) the rugged upper slopes of these windswept Lakeland hills are open and bare.

## DERBYSHIRE VILLAGES

Much of Derbyshire falls within the hill country which falls away from the Peak near the Yorkshire border and forms the southern end of the long Pennine Chain. Most of the villages are in the valleys, including those of the Dove and Derwent, many of them tiny hamlets; but there are a few larger ones, such as Hartington (*below*). Only a few lie on the high ground separating the valleys. Among these latter is Tissington. Its church has much medieval workmanship, including the beautifully moulded Norman window shown (*left*). It is one of the best known of Derbyshire villages, partly on account of the traditional custom of well-dressing, which takes place on the day before Good Friday, in thanksgiving, it is said, for the purity of the water which allowed Tissington to escape the ravages of a great medieval plague. Whether in the valleys or on the uplands, the Derbyshire villages are mainly stone-built with material drawn from the local quarries, although modern re-housing in brick has sounded a rather discordant note in some of the larger villages.

## VISITOR'S BRIDGE, DOVEDALE

ANOTHER of Dovedale's beautifully situated villages is shown here. The narrow old bridge over the river is called Visitor's Bridge and, like much of Dovedale, is in the keeping of the National Trust. The photograph illustrates well the tendency of all the villages in the limestone valleys to be built at the point where a transverse valley meets the main valley. Dovedale itself, like the upper reaches of the Yorkshire dales, is often so narrow and inaccessible that it defied the foundation of early settlements, except where the junction of two valleys gave room for development. Here the cottages straggle up a narrow road closely hemmed in by the frowning hills to a group of farm buildings seen in the middle distance. Stone walls climb to the very summits of the tree-girt hills, in contrast with the scene in Lakeland where only sparse vegetation grows above the lower slopes (see page 59).

## SCENES FROM THE DALES

THROUGH the dales of Derbyshire and Yorkshire, farms and villages are scattered thinly. In severe winters communities may be cut off for a time from the outside world. So the dalesmen are self-reliant people. The village school and the village shop, which often stocks a very wide range of goods and attends as well to post-office and savings-bank business, are centres of prime importance. Major influence on the life of these communities is exerted also by some individuals, the local craftsmen. The value of the weaver, whether making fabrics, like the man on the left, or cattle bands, like the weaver from Hawes on the

right, or of the cobbler, is obvious. Though the work of another craftsman, the dry-stone waller, can be seen everywhere in the dales where the walls replace the hedgerows common in other parts of England, the high degree of skill needed to fit together large stones without the aid of mortar to make a solid wall is not always realized. That these walls should endure the rigours of the seasons, and often the strain of leaning cattle within the fields they surround, says much for the craftsmanship of such dalesmen as the one pictured below, who has been dry-walling for many years, using the local limestone, which is more durable than any hedge.

## COXWOLD, VILLAGE OF THE HILLS

ALTHOUGH most of Yorkshire's famous villages are situated in the dales or on the rocky coastline, there is also a number of distinctive and charming places in the rolling uplands which lie to the east of the Great North Road between the Vale of York and the coast. Coxwold, pictured here, is one of these, on the road from Boroughbridge to Helmsley. It is on the fringe of the North York Moors, in an area memorable by reason of the great abbeys of Byland and Rievaulx, which were among the wealthiest of the medieval foundations. Coxwold is pleasantly built on two low ridges and in the valley between them, which is well wooded by contrast with the bare slopes of the neighbouring hills. This photograph shows how greatly the beauty of the place is enhanced by the mature trees which almost hide the fine Gothic church on the hill beyond. It was here that Laurence Sterne was incumbent between 1760 and his death in 1768. Most of *Tristram Shandy* and the whole of his *A Sentimental Journey Through France and Italy* were penned in the parish.

## WEST TANFIELD ON THE URE

MANY of Yorkshire's most attractive villages are in the dales, a series of long valleys which pierce the eastern slopes of the Pennine Chain. Some of those high up the dales are illustrated on later pages. West Tanfield, shown here, lies beside the Ure, the river of Wensleydale, near the point where it enters the Plain of York, a slow, placid stream in contrast with the rushing torrent into which it turns after heavy rain in its upper reaches. The stone fabric of the houses, the church and the castle are reflected in the clear water of the river. This is a village which has a true unity derived from its compactness and the uniform building stone which appears in all its old buildings. It has the added quality of representing at a single glance the essential parts of a medieval village from the time of the Saxon kings to Tudor days—the church, the old cottages and the castle or manor-house.

### BAINBRIDGE IN WENSLEYDALE

IN THE heart of a valley which is one of the richest in all the Pennine country, Bainbridge shares with Kettlewell (*opposite*) all the best features of the villages of the Yorkshire dales. Almost every house and cottage is built of locally quarried stone; the bridge, too, is of stone; the river which flows beneath it and is depicted above in full spate is the River Bain.

# IN THE YORKSHIRE DALES

IN the midst of the wild Pennine country the barren moors throw into sharp relief the kinder and more fertile mood of the valleys, and this epitomizes the spirit of welcome which is a very real thing to the traveller who toils over the grass-covered ridges and comes at last to the point where he sees the valley spread out below him. Kettlewell is a village near the head of Wharfedale. It lies farther within the massif of the Pennines than does Bainbridge, shown on the page opposite, and consequently it resembles even more clearly an oasis in the desert land. Its narrow strip of cultivated soil is marked out into fields by the stone walls which are universal in the region. It lies close to the ridges which come down from Penyghent and Whernside, two of the highest points in the Pennine Chain. In recent years, particularly since walking holidays in the Pennines have become popular, Kettlewell has been one of the favourite centres from which to explore the grand country around Whernside.

# AN OLD-WORLD CUSTOM AT WHITBY

WHITBY retains in the custom of "planting the penny hedge" a tradition of great antiquity. The legend is that knights hunting wild boar pursued their quarry into the abbey chapel and there slaughtered the boar and also a monk who tried to prevent them from thus desecrating holy ground. A penance was imposed upon them and their heirs, requiring them to build a hedge of wicker on a spot called Abraham's Bosom on the bank of the River Esk, to be of sufficient strength to withstand seven tides and to cost no more than the sum of a penny. The penalty is still noted in the deeds of the land. In this recent picture the land-holders are building the hedge while a representative of the lord of the manor blows an ancient hunting horn and repeats the words of the monk: "Out on ye, out on ye, out on ye."

## STAITHES, IN THE NORTH RIDING

THERE are a number of quaint and attractive villages along the coast of Yorkshire's North Riding between Scarborough and Saltburn. Staithes, pictured here, is only a few miles from the manufacturing town of Loftus and is set in the midst of the final and most northerly phase of Yorkshire's wild and rugged cliff scenery. In spite of its proximity to the iron-works and the shipbuilding industries of Tees-side, it remains as secluded a village as any along the coast, precluded by its position under the beetling cliffs from rapid expansion, its fishermen's cottages picturesquely grouped round the tiny river which flows here into the sea and forms a natural harbour for the fishing-boats. As befits a village dependent on the sea for its existence, Staithes has a coastguard station and a long history. It was here that James Cook, the famous eighteenth-century navigator, whose name will be always associated with Australia, was apprenticed and from here he ran away to sea.

## VILLAGES OF THE PLAIN AND MOOR

CATTERICK (*above*) and Goathland (*below*) are villages which represent the two most diverse elements of the North Riding of Yorkshire. Catterick, with its pleasant green and charming medieval church, is typical of the many prosperous villages which are situated in the plain between the outliers of the Pennine Chain and the Cleveland Hills. It lies on the River Swale below Richmond, just before it enters the broad Vale of York. Many of the villages of the Vale of York are reminiscent of south-country villages. They have the same tradition of a long agricultural history and are the last strongholds in the north of a dying feudalism. Goathland, by contrast, is set high amid the North York Moors, a few miles inland from Robin Hood's Bay. The wild moorland scenery gives the village its special character as an oasis in the midst of a countryside which, in spite of its verdant appearance, has a shallow subsoil that has defied the people of all ages to cultivate it.

ROBIN HOOD'S BAY, YORKSHIRE

ROSTHWAITE IN BORROWDALE: THE PEAKS INCLUDE GLARAMARA

GREAT END, SCAFELL PIKE, GREAT GABLE AND GREEN GABLE

73

WHITCHURCH, OXFORDSHIRE

74

# The Midlands

THE Midland belt of England includes two areas which are by virtue of their scenery and tradition especially dear to the hearts of all country lovers. These are Shakespeare's country with the Forest of Arden, and the country of the hunting shires.

Charming country nearly always begets charming villages. Especially is this true of well-wooded upland country in which the timbered hills always form a background for the village vistas, and there are usually trees within the confines of the village itself to give it added attraction. It would be surprising, therefore, if the Midlands of England did not have a wealth of varied village beauty. There are indeed many village groups in almost all the Midland counties away from the great industrial complex to gladden the heart of any artist and fit to be compared with many of the more famous villages of southern England.

There is not, of course, in all the Midlands any village settlement with the fascination of the smaller and quainter villages of Devon and Cornwall. That is inevitable, because the latter depend to an imponderable but certainly large degree on their situation as seaside villages nestling under cliffs. Take away the sea and the cliffs and there would be much less that is remarkable about them. The Midlands have, however, a group of villages on much the same lines as Gloucestershire's famous Cotswold villages. The Wold spills over into Oxfordshire, and many of the Oxfordshire villages such as Great Tew, Churchill and Minster Lovell rank high among the illustrious villages of the Wold. Some may say that this is a case of the Midlands stealing the thunder of the West Country. So be it. Let us admit that Oxfordshire Wold villages belong more to the West than to the Midlands.

That cannot be true of the long line of hills which is so closely related to the Cotswolds and which extends through Northamptonshire and Leicestershire. The rolling uplands in both counties conceal hundreds of tiny villages within their folds, many of them stone-built like the Cotswold villages, and built, of course, of the same stone, the oolitic limestone which forms the substratum of all this countryside. Two that, once visited, are long remembered include Knossington, a hilltop village overlooking Rutland's fertile Vale of Catmose, and Launde, more a scattered collection of charming old buildings than a village in the proper sense of the word. There are many others, all of them lying so far off the beaten track that they are rarely visited by strangers and are known only to the rural communities born and bred in this distinctive countryside.

Away to the south of Northampton's hill country the land slopes towards the valley of the Ouse, which is the parent river of the Midland Plain and fittingly has along its banks a number of entirely charming places with all the attraction of riverside villages and a personality of their own as well. Most famous of a proud line is Olney, its stone-spired church a famous landmark in the countryside of the Ouse. Unlike most of the remote places of the Midlands, it has become a centre visited by the people of Northampton and other industrial towns. That cannot be said of several other villages only a few miles away, such as Turvey and Newton Blossomville, the latter one of the prettiest villages in all England.

Lower downstream, where the waterway of the Ouse broadens into a slow-moving river of infinite dignity, it has on its banks old towns such as Huntingdon and St. Ives, and many villages, including Hemingford Grey, which is just as entrancing as the better-known ones higher upstream. One could not fairly omit the villages of the Ouse Valley from any grouping of England's loveliest places.

Some think of Warwickshire as all Birmingham. Certainly that great and still-growing city is not precisely an encouragement for old and tiny places to retain that air of seclusion which adds immeasurably to village character. Nevertheless, just as many of the villages of the Home Counties within thirty miles of London are comparatively unspoilt, so many of the villages of Warwickshire within fifteen or twenty miles of Birmingham's outskirts seem to have avoided the flow of people and of traffic alike and to lie just as much off the beaten track as though they were a hundred miles away from the nearest town.

The popularity of the Great Bard brings tens of thousands every year to Stratford-upon-Avon, but there are many quiet villages within a few miles of the town centre. Bidford-on-Avon demands recognition; even Shottery, virtually a suburb of Stratford, is still a village in its own right; while the villages of the Forest of Arden, such as Maxstoke-in-Arden and the most famous and largest of them all, Henley-in-Arden, are distinctive and distinguished by the number of half-timbered and thatched cottages and small houses which they retain from a more gracious age of village architecture. The half-timbered style is given added beauty here by the thick thatches which are still kept in repair and renewed when necessary, defying ugly modern roof materials to oust them from their rightful place. Some of the new cottages are being thatched here as they are in Norfolk —a pleasant if sometimes self-conscious anachronism.

Finally, one other group of villages deserves a word and still more a visit. That is the group which clusters round the sandstone hills that lie in Bedfordshire between the valley of the Ouse and the downs of Dunstable. Woburn is a place of many gracious Georgian houses. Aspley Guise, Bow Brickhill and a number of others, in a lovely setting of parklands and pine woods, are all, like Woburn, in the tradition of Georgian villages, a real link between the rare charm of the medieval settlement and the hackneyed and dull ideas of Victorian and later builders.

## WELFORD-ON-AVON

THE valley of the River Avon reveals some of the most attractive Midland scenery and some of the most fascinating of its villages. Here at Welford, where the river flows through gentle Warwickshire meadows, there are the heavily thatched and half-timbered cottages which belong specially to England's river valleys, where there was always an abundant supply of timber for building purposes and reeds for thatching could be gathered in the marshland near the river's course before modern draining of the land was brought to perfection. The tradition in village architecture, so happily set by the builders of Tudor and Elizabethan days, persisted through the following centuries. In the modern age, when brick has become the most popular and, in many districts, the only material for building new cottages (except where there is an abundant supply of local stone), a growing consciousness of the beauty of old cottages has allowed what is ancient to be preserved and often repaired with loving care. This village group, with the graceful Gothic tower of the church in the background and the carefully tended lawn which fronts the charming old cottages with their diamond-paned windows, is like a page from a book of seventeenth-century England.

## OLD CUSTOMS IN MIDLAND VILLAGES

HALLATON, near Market Harborough, and Ilmington, nine miles from Shakespeare's birthplace at Stratford-upon-Avon, are linked together because of old customs of a very different kind which each preserves. Barrel kicking, or playing a kind of football with a barrel instead of a ball (*opposite*), at Hallaton is a revival of an age-old custom, maintained now with as much enthusiasm as ever. The fiddler of Ilmington (*above*) is a traditional figure in the life of his village; an authority on English folk-lore who, when this photograph was taken, had been fiddling or leading the dancing on May Days, at Harvest Homes and other village celebrations for more than half a century. The fiddler's regalia of smock, beflowered hat, multi-coloured garters and bells has been known to three generations of village people. Like others associated with the traditions of folk-lore and country dancing, this old man of Ilmington had a tremendous repertoire and had played from memory more than a hundred tunes in a single day, many of them passed down by ear from father to son for hundreds of years, as in the days of the medieval minstrels, but never committed to paper. Nowadays there are many societies for the purpose of preserving the form and spirit of country dancing and the associated morris dancing which was introduced into England about 1350. But there are still happily a great number of villages in which the people dance in their folk traditions spontaneously as the special celebrations in the rural calendar.

## WEST OF THE FENS

WEST of the Fen country, in the higher reaches of the Ouse Valley and near the borders of Huntingdonshire and Northamptonshire, the land, intensively cultivated from Saxon times, was unusually rich so that the villages on it prospered. Godmanchester (*left*) is one of these villages on the banks of the Ouse opposite Huntingdon and astride the Roman road from London to York. Lowick in Northampton (*below*) is on the high ground above the Nene. The outbuildings of the manor-farm make a striking foreground for the elaborately decorated tower of the parish church with its multiple weather-vanes set on the pinnacles.

## IN OLD ELSTOW

ELSTOW in Bedfordshire is John Bunyan's village. The great author was the son of an Elstow tradesman. He continued to live there for the whole of his early life. *The Pilgrim's Progress* was written partly while he was imprisoned in the gaol at near-by Bedford Bridge. The moot hall at Elstow (*right*) is on the village green where Bunyan was wont to play as a child. It is a fine example of sixteenth-century domestic architecture. May Day is still celebrated at Elstow in the traditional style. The colourful procession (*below*), composed largely of children preceding and following the "royal carriage," is on its way to the green to crown the May Queen.

HEMINGFORD GREY ON THE BANKS OF THE OUSE

82

## KIMBOLTON, HUNTINGDONSHIRE

THE broad main street of Kimbolton widens into something akin to a market square between the lofty spire of the parish church and the entrance to the castle at its other end. In the twentieth century Kimbolton has slipped back into the peace and quiet of a typical English rural settlement. Its medieval importance was due to its castle, which became a famous mansion at a time when most of the English castles were decayed. It reached the zenith of its fame at the beginning of the eighteenth century when the old castle palace was rebuilt by Sir John Vanbrugh, the architect who designed Blenheim Palace. Many of the fine Georgian houses in the main street were built about this time. The tapering stone spire of the church is a fine medieval example of a type which is a marked local feature of the many attractive churches of the valley of the Ouse and the surrounding countryside. Kimbolton Castle has its own special place in history as the home of Catherine of Aragon at the time of her death in 1536. It was to Kimbolton that she retired after her divorce from Henry VIII. During the time between her divorce and her death it is recorded that she lived the life of a near-recluse within the confines of the castle and as a devout Roman Catholic devoted her remaining days to an exacting and most austere religious régime

## VILLAGES OF NORTHAMPTONSHIRE

LESS well known than those of the southern counties or of the Cotswolds, the villages of Northamptonshire include a few that are unusually interesting and distinguished. The three shown on these pages are in a similar tradition, though each shows a special feature. The single facet which links them together is the locally quarried stone. In this respect the villages of Northamptonshire are related inevitably to those of the Cotswold country, if it is remembered that an extension of the Cotswold range crosses the county from west to east from the region of Daventry to Rockingham Forest on the borders of Rutland. This rolling upland countryside is rich in ironstone, from which the county's mineral wealth is derived, and yields also a bountiful supply of building stone similar in texture and colour to that of the Cotswold stone itself. Because the rest of Northamptonshire is deficient in building materials, medieval builders and to some extent more recent ones transported the stone from the quarries in the hills into every corner of the county. Geddington (*left*) is a quiet village five miles from Kettering. In this picture are shown some of the stone-built houses acting as a frame for the Gothic tower and spire of the parish church and for the Eleanor Cross, one of the twelve or more crosses set up by Edward I along the road taken by the funeral cortege of his wife, Eleanor. Rockingham (*top, right*) is set on the edge of the limestone ridge and commands a wonderful view over the lowlands beyond. Almost every cottage here is stone-built and many of them are thatched. The ancient cottages and ford (*bottom, right*) are at Dodford, a village situated a few miles to the east of Daventry.

84

## ON THE EDGE OF THE FENS

THE villages of the Cambridgeshire Fens, and indeed of the whole expanse of the Fen country, are completely unlike the traditional idea of an English village. They are mainly nineteenth-century settlements strung out along the roads with very little beauty and no special interest. Medieval villages are, of course, entirely absent because in the Middle Ages the Fen country was unreclaimed and uninhabited. On the edges of the Fens, however, there are many pleasant villages dating from the time when they were like oases in a wilderness of swamp. The thatched roof is a feature of many of them because of the ample supply of reeds that could be gathered in the marshy land. Swaffham Prior (*above*), well known for its unusual church tower, and Wicken (*below*), on the edge of Wicken Fen, are two in the district which have definite character and a real old-world charm.

## VILLAGES OF OXFORDSHIRE

OXFORDSHIRE shares in three distinct and distinctive types of countryside and has within its boundaries villages which take their character from each of the three scenic types. The Cotswold country in the west crosses the county boundary from Gloucestershire. Great Tew (*right*) is one of the most colourful and ancient of the villages in this area. Then there is the valley of the Thames, with its quiet riverside villages. The third type is represented by the flint-built villages which are found in the Chilterns.

## OXFORDSHIRE VILLAGE IN THE THAMES VALLEY

CLIFTON HAMPDEN (*below*) lies in the Thames Valley between Abingdon and Dorchester.

# COURTYARD OF A COACHING INN

The old inns of England are a vivid and enduring link with English social life through the ages. There are many inns at least three hundred or four hundred years old and a few much older than that. Often when the front of an inn is rebuilt or modern extensions are added parts of the old building are deliberately preserved as a link with its long history. The coaching inns have a special fascination. This photograph is of George Yard at Burford in Oxfordshire, formerly the courtyard of the George Inn, one of the oldest inns of England, with a history of centuries of hospitality before the great era of coaching days, when it achieved its greatest fame. Burford itself is a small town rather than a village, though it has many of the qualities of a village. Several of the building styles which give it its diversity are represented in this picture—the steep-pitched eaves of Tudor origin, the overhanging upper storey which continued to distinguish houses and cottages alike in the seventeenth century, and, through the arch, a graceful Georgian doorway flanked by classical columns in the style which made the eighteenth-century architecture of England so memorable.

## SHOTTERY, NEAR STRATFORD

SHOTTERY village is no more than a mile from the centre of Stratford-upon-Avon, yet it retains to a remarkable degree its character as an independent village, defying the twentieth century to make it into a suburb of Stratford. It has preserved, in however diminished form, its village green and pond, its own village shops, a number of old cottages which date from the time of Shakespeare, and incidentally a manor-house which has preserved its great hall and much of the appearance of an ancient manor in spite of modern additions. This well-maintained row of old cottages faces the green. The end one nearest the camera illustrates the medieval crock construction with shaped beams supporting the steeply pitched roof. This is a traditional style of cottage building, well seen also at Lacock in Wiltshire, current in the sixteenth and seventeenth centuries, but generally replaced in the course of time or covered over with a new facing. Shottery has one other building of national fame, the cottage in which Anne Hathaway, Shakespeare's wife, was born and bred. Not only is the exterior of the cottage much as in Anne's time, but much of the interior fittings and furniture belong to the cottage as it was in the sixteenth century.

LUCCOMBE, IN THE SOMERSET HILLS

# The West
# and South-west

ROM the Cotswold country to the Land's End peninsula, from the Wye
Valley to the valleys of Shropshire, the villages of the west and south-west,
if not quite so varied as those of south-eastern England, are certainly as
distinctive, and though not quite so numerous are at least as picturesque. Many
artists and writers have chosen the villages of the Cotswold countryside as the
typical villages of rural England. Certainly they stand high among the loveliest
groups of villages in the country and have an unusually well-defined character.

The one quality which gives all the Cotswold villages unity and makes them
without the slightest doubt members of the same family is the universal use of the
local building stone, the oolitic limestone which colours the rural landscapes of
the area and gives tone to cottage, farmhouse and church alike.

The Cotswold country in medieval days was very prosperous because, like
Suffolk and Kent, it was one of the chief sheep-rearing areas of Britain. That
rural prosperity has been handed down through generations and has been renewed
because of the richness of the soil in the valleys. The consequence is that many of
the Cotswold villages are unusually well set-up and handsomely built. There are
many fine fifteenth-century churches similar to those of Suffolk and Kent, but
built of the same local stone as the smallest cottage. In the larger villages there are
fine merchants' houses dating from the fifteenth and sixteenth centuries and farmhouses and manor-houses of about the same period.

The local stone weathers quickly to a mellow grey and is still used largely for
building purposes in place of the otherwise ubiquitous brick. The result is that
the shock of transition from the old to the new which spoils the view of so many
villages in the east is almost entirely absent in the Wold, where the traditional
aspect of a feudal village is jealously maintained.

Some of the Cotswold villages have, in addition, very real beauty of situation
or composition, especially along the valleys of the Windrush and Coln. Bibury,
Lower Slaughter, Bourton-on-the-Water, Broadway at the northern extremity of
the Wold, stand out in the memory. To that list perhaps there ought to be added
the names of Chipping Campden and Stow-on-the-Wold, though these are small
towns rather than villages.

If the Cotswold villages stand out in the West Country, the fishing villages of
Cornwall are equally distinguished in their very different way. These are mostly

ancient settlements set round a tiny haven or straggling down a narrow gully, the homes of fisherfolk for more than a thousand years and remarkably little changed in the last century of so-called progress. In fact they are not likely to change, since the situation of many of them is such that new building, except at a distance, is utterly impossible. Any extension of Port Isaac must be, as it has been in the past, on the cliff top in a position happily out of sight of the village itself.

The same is true to a lesser extent of Polperro and Mevagissey and the villages on the south of Land's End peninsula from Mousehole to Lamorna and Sennen Cove. A few such as Porthallow and Porthoustock can only be approached by an uncommonly steep hill. Others, like St. Mawes in the Roseland peninsula, are at the end of long roads which branch off from the few main roads in Cornwall and are too far from the arteries of commerce to attract major new development.

Unlike those of southern and eastern England, the villages of Cornwall's hinterland have a Celtic tradition and straggle along the roads without any of the compactness or grace which characterize the feudal village of Saxon England.

Across the borders of Devonshire, however, many of the little settlements around Dartmoor have much of the attractiveness of a feudal village, with the added beauty of a superb situation. There can be few villages in the whole world more happily placed than Widecombe in a deep hollow under the frowning moorlands of Dartmoor, or Buckland amid the dense wood of Holne Chase. The coastal villages of Devonshire, too, vie with those of Cornwall in their quaintness and their beauty. Clovelly and Lynmouth in the north, Hope and Salcombe in the south, are all claimants to a place in Britain's hundred most beautiful villages.

There is, perhaps, nothing especially distinctive in the villages of Somerset and Dorset, though the latter county includes several in the troughs of the chalk downland which are at least as attractive places as the hill villages of the south-east. Cerne Abbas and Sydling St. Nicholas and, nearer the coast, Little Bredy and Abbotsbury and Corfe—every one of them has points of exceptional charm.

For sheer distinction of architectural style the villages of the Marcher counties take pride of place, especially those of Herefordshire and Shropshire. All this was well-wooded country in the sixteenth and seventeenth centuries, so timber, as in Essex, was the natural material for building. Some quirk of local inspiration produced the curious half-timbered style which is always picturesque and sometimes arresting in its unusual beauty. The style in its most developed form is known as magpie architecture; in its simplest it is very like the half-timbered building of the Midlands and East Anglia. There is so much of it in the Marcher counties, in the big towns as well as the villages, in the farmhouses and manor-houses as well as in the cottages, that it gives the whole of these counties a special character, best seen perhaps in some of the larger villages like Weobley. It is rarely absent from any village which retains old houses. That means almost all in the two counties.

BEER, DEVONSHIRE, PHOTOGRAPHED FROM THE CHALK CLIFFS

## FAIRFORD, ON A TRIBUTARY OF THE THAMES

THERE are numerous old-world villages in the upper valley of the Thames, which rises near Seven Springs in the Cotswolds and flows down a narrow defile which broadens round Lechlade and Faringdon until the valley of the Thames is lost in the vast tract of level country known as White Horse Vale  Fairford is the first of the large villages on the Coln, a tributary which joins it at Lechlade. The church, here photographed from the farther bank of the river, is an architectural gem in the tradition of the late Gothic churches so common in the West Country. It was built in 1493 and is specially famous for its series of stained-glass windows, among the finest medieval glass in the country. They depict the story of the Creation and the work of Jesus Christ. Once it was thought that they were imported; certainly they show all the signs of early Flemish workmanship; but now it is generally believed that they were prepared by English craftsmen under Flemish tutors.

## NORTHLEACH, GLOUCESTERSHIRE

IT has often been noted how admirably stone-built Cotswold villages and towns blend with the countryside. This photograph of Northleach, which is near the centre of the Wold proper and on the high road which links Cheltenham with Witney, confirms the impression vividly. The generous woodlands serve as a pleasant background for a scene in which Nature and man have combined to convey the essence of the English countryside through the medium of a composition which builds up admirably to the elegant tall-towered church. That there is not a single discordant note in the whole picture is due in part to the fact that the village is built throughout of the local limestone, the same stone that makes up the buildings and the walls in the middle distance and determines the colouring of the land itself. The straight lines of the parish church accentuated by the bold perpendicular tracery of the windows are similar to those of Fairford (*opposite*), though on a more elaborate scale.

## COTSWOLD VILLAGES

THE smaller villages of the Cotswold country are just as attractive as larger ones such as Northleach (page 95). Three of the most interesting are pictured on these pages, all of them (like most of the villages of the Wold) set in one or other of the gentle river valleys which break up the high ground into a succession of ridges and intervening hollows. Bibury (*above*) is in the valley of the Coln, in the midst of the rolling countryside which lies between Burford and the valley of the Thames. The row of stone-built cottages in the foreground is known as Arlington Row, as perfect a group of medieval cottages in stone as those pictured on page 89 are of half-timbered ones. On the page opposite are the two Slaughter villages, Upper Slaughter (*above*) and Lower Slaughter (*below*), which depend on their river setting and the graceful well-grown trees which add tone to the village scene for much of their beauty. For the rest, both these villages show the same harmonious quality as Bibury, a quality inherent in the warm grey stone which gives its own beauty.

## CRAFTSMEN OF THE WEST COUNTRY

IT IS often stated that craftsmanship is dying out in face of competition from factory products. That is clearly true so far as many former rural industries are concerned. Even in an era of highly mechanized and standardized production, however, there are still many rural occupations demanding a high quality of personal craftsmanship—and still a number of rural industries in which the machine can never entirely supplant individual workmanship. A few of the highly specialized crafts of the West Country are illustrated on these pages. The West Country has always been the stronghold of tradition; it remains the area of Britain in which craftsmanship has survived most vigorously. (*Top, left*), at Mortehoe, in North Devon, a farmer prepares to clip a sheep with hand shears. This method is but rarely used now; where electric power is not available the shears usually are worked by a flexible drive from a

wheel rotated by hand. (*Bottom, left*), a Devon fisherman is constructing a crab-pot. Fishing has for centuries been the principal industry of many of the coastal villages of both Devon and Cornwall. The village blacksmith shown (*bottom, centre*) is at Widecombe-in-the-Moor. The moor, of course, is Dartmoor, and this particular forge is by tradition the one at which the horse of the Uncle Tom Cobbleigh of the famous song was shod. On this page are depicted two equally famous but widely diverse activities. (*Right*), a lacemaker is at work at Honiton, in Devon, a village of which the name has become a hallmark for a certain kind of lace. (*Below*), apples are being loaded into a cider press at Newent, in Gloucestershire. Cider is made throughout the West Country both by individual farmers and by firms specializing in bulk production. There are very many kinds of cider, bottled and draught. Some are dry, some sweet, and one or more of them are pleasing to most palates.

## ON THE BORDERS OF WALES

LLANOVER stands posed between the tumbled hills and valleys of England and the bare
Black Mountains of Wales. The battlemented tower of its tiny church is graceful as well
as ancient, so are some of the cottages which lie between it and the placid waterway of the
Usk. But the whole character of the place derives from its wonderful situation rather than
from any product of man's handiwork, ancient or modern. Nowhere is the contrast between
the peace of the English landscape and the grandeur of the typical Welsh one more clearly
illustrated. Even though Monmouthshire is in many ways akin to Wales, this part of the
Usk Valley near Abergavenny is still as English in scenic tradition as the valleys of the
south country, with its green level meadows, its scattered clumps of willows and elms
and oaks, and the riverside village nestling among them. The bare slopes of the mountains
in the background extend to the uplands of central Wales and the Brecon Beacons.

## VILLAGES OF THE MARCHER COUNTRY

MUCH WENLOCK in Shropshire (*right*) and Weobley in Herefordshire (*below*) have many examples of the elaborate half-timbered style of domestic architecture which is a conspicuous part of the historic heritage of the Marcher counties. The decorative guildhall of Much Wenlock is raised above the old market place on pillars, which records show were once used as whipping posts when local jurisdiction was truly summary. The date of the guildhall is the latter part of the sixteenth century. Some of the timbered houses with overhanging upper storeys in Weobley are probably about a century later, though there is a tradition that the house on the extreme left of the picture was the home of a merchant in Tudor times.

CHILDS WICKHAM, WORCESTERSHIRE

## BROADWAY, WORCESTERSHIRE

MOST famous and probably most frequented of all the stone-built villages in and near the Cotswolds, Broadway is a long, straggling place built on either side of the main road from Oxford to Worcester. Its special attraction derives from two factors, first the graceful architecture of its houses and cottages, many of which date from the fifteenth and sixteenth centuries and are almost without exception stone-built, and secondly from its setting immediately beneath the steeply rising slopes of the Wold itself, which can be seen in the background of this photograph. This is one of the highest parts of the Cotswolds, exceeding one thousand feet at the beacon tower which is built on the summit a little to the right of the picture. The village belongs to a part of Worcestershire which extends in a narrow belt into Gloucestershire so that the county boundary is only about two miles away in any direction save due north. Its name is not, as many writers have stated, derived from the broad main street; the latter was constructed only in the fifteenth century when the route between London and Worcester was re-aligned, and the village itself was founded at least four hundred years before that. Among the many fine buildings, the Lygon Arms, pictured on the left of this photograph, an old posting inn, and the meeting place of the local hunt, stands out on account of its age and the fine graceful lines of its architecture. Some of its present fabric and the greater part of its ground plan belong to the sixteenth century.

## VILLAGE CONTRASTS IN DORSET

OKEFORD FITZPAINE (*left*) and Abbotsbury (*below*) lie on either side of the Dorset Downs, the former sheltered under their northern edge and looking to the fertile Vale of Blackmore, the latter between the southern escarpment of the hills and the sea. Okeford Fitzpaine has the half-timbered cottages that belong to the well-wooded valley, Abbotsbury is stone-built. Both are attractive and harmonize perfectly with their surroundings, but whereas Okeford is a little village which has always lived as a small self-contained agricultural community, Abbotsbury is a large village or small town with a proud history. Its medieval tithe barn and a ruined chapel recall the time when its monastery was one of the richest in southern England.

## LYME REGIS FROM THE COBB

LYME REGIS is two places in one: a small and compact watering-place, fairly modern in appearance though not in tradition, here seen in the background of the picture, and, an almost separate entity, a fishing village by the cobb or breakwater which shelters the harbour.

## UNDER THE SHADOW OF A MEDIEVAL CASTLE

CORFE CASTLE is the name of the castle and of the village under its shadow, a pretty stone-built village with some charming medieval and Georgian houses built in the same local material as the castle itself. The castle guards the only pass through the Purbeck Hills and stands on a promontory of the chalk downs dominating both the pass itself and the valley which stretches away toward Wareham. There is a tradition of a Saxon castle on the same site, where it is said Edward the Martyr, King of Saxon England, was staying when he was murdered on the order of his stepmother, Elfrida. The Normans could not neglect such a commanding site. They built a new castle from which date some of the present ruins, which are mainly of the thirteenth century. A village soon began to grow up under the protection of the castle. Though the castle suffered the usual fate of fortresses in southern England and was dismantled by the victorious forces of Cromwell at the end of the Civil War, the village continued to thrive and has had a continuous and prosperous history.

## VILLAGES OF THE DOWNS

CERNE ABBAS (*right*) and Little Bredy (*below*) are both set in the midst of the magnificent scenery of the Dorset Downs. Cerne Abbas is an ancient place which had fame in the Middle Ages because of the wealth of its monastic foundation, the church of which is still in service as the parish church. Today Cerne is the largest village in the downland country, a shopping centre for the many tiny villages within a radius of ten miles, and is full of graceful seventeenth-century houses and cottages. Little Bredy is a complete contrast, a tiny settlement in a deep combe of the hills centred round the manor-farm and cottages and so secluded that it is rarely chanced upon by casual way-farers, a little world of its own in the true English village tradition.

## COMBE MARTIN, NORTH DEVON

THIS arresting photograph from the air demonstrates how villages along the rocky coasts of south-western England have been forced by the terrain to spread inland from the coast along narrow valleys which end in a natural anchorage. Today Combe Martin is nearly two miles long and never more than a quarter of a mile broad, its outer limits set by the steep slopes of the hills which rise quickly to an elevation of nearly a thousand feet.

## MILTON ABBAS

LIKE Combe Martin (*opposite*), Milton Abbas, Dorset, straggles along the trough of a deep valley cut into the hills. It is a model of late eighteenth-century village planning, the road bordered by a grassy fringe and each cottage having its own large garden stretching up the hillside. A vacant patch of grassy land separates each pair of cottages. The whole village represents an ideal of the first Earl of Dorchester, which has been fully realized.

## ANCIENT VILLAGES OF EAST DEVON

THE Devon countryside east of the Exe is relatively unknown compared with the more spectacular landscapes of central Devonshire and the South Hams, yet it is as interesting as any in the West Country. The villages pictured on these pages, Otterton (*left*), Budleigh Salterton (*below*) and East Budleigh (*opposite*), are all within a radius of five miles, but, as these photographs show, reveal many of the most attractive phases of village architecture. The thatched and white-washed cottages of Otterton date mainly from the seventeenth century. They are given added character by the little stream which runs between them and the road. The group of graceful houses in Budleigh Salterton has the fascination of Georgian architecture, while at East Budleigh is an unusually handsome medieval village church in which are a number of monuments linking it with Sir Walter Raleigh, who was born at Hayes Barton, a short distance away.

## VILLAGES IN A VALLEY

IN A hill country like the greater part of Devonshire, intensive agriculture from the Middle Ages to the present day has been possible only in the valleys, where, as a result, almost all the villages are situated. Widecombe-in-the-Moor (*left*) and Branscombe (*below*) are both valley villages, sheltered by high surrounding hills, the centres of a flourishing but limited agriculture. In the case of Widecombe the fields rise quickly to the outliers of Dartmoor, where the magnificent tower of Widecombe Church is a far-seen landmark. This village is the scene of Widecombe Fair, celebrated in traditional song and, still held in September, a sheep fair of more than local importance. Branscombe lies in one of the steep valleys which run to the coast near the Dorset boundary.

## RIVERSIDE VILLAGES

OF DEVONSHIRE'S many riverside villages those along the River Dart are especially lovely, among them Dittisham (*right*); a collection of old-world houses dominated by the battlemented tower of the parish church, the little street slopes steeply to the banks of the wide river. Newton Ferrers (*below*) is one of a number of villages close by the banks of the Yealm in a wonderfully secluded situation, sheltered alike by the rolling hills and the abundant woodlands near the river. Though many of its dwelling-places are modern, the village group, which builds up toward the square-towered church, with the hill behind and the placid waterway dotted with pleasure-boats in the foreground, is as happy a composition as any devised by man in these parts.

"HOT MONEY" CEREMONY ON FAIR DAY AT HONITON, DEVON

BEATING THE BOUNDS AT PLYMSTOCK, DEVON

## EXMOOR VILLAGE

THE Exmoor countryside, for all its wild heather-covered hills and long empty vistas, is essentially civilized, with wooded slopes and green fields, which are never far from the grandeur of the moorland scenery. Just as the southern fringe of Dartmoor conceals many of Devonshire's loveliest villages, so the southern fringe of Exmoor contains a number of green and charming valleys, each with its compact and isolated village, of which Winsford (*above*) is one of the most justly famous, though Simonsbath and Withypool and Exford are three others within a radius of ten miles which have an equal fascination and no less beauty of architecture. Winsford Church with its battlemented tower seems to stand guard over the small village which is contained rigidly within its medieval boundaries. Many of its cottages are still thatched and the life of the people is concerned almost solely with working the land. Winsford used to be a favourite meeting place for the Exmoor stag-hounds, which found their quarry among the woods and heather commons of the surrounding hills. It stands on both banks of the infant River Exe which passes on its swift downward course through the centre of the village. The photograph was taken from the heather slopes of the upstanding hill dividing this valley from its neighbour, that of the Barle, which can be reached by footpath across the moors to Tarr Steps, a spot less than four miles from Winsford Church, where the river can be crossed on stepping-stones.

## DUNSTER, SOMERSET

The high ridge of Exmoor separates Dunster (*above*) from Winsford (*opposite*). Dunster's medieval fame arose from its pre-eminence as a market centre for Somerset woollen cloth. Its modern fame is expressed in the thousands of pictures by artists and photographers, which reproduce the spirit of timeless beauty epitomized in the gabled yarn market, the rows of attractive dwelling-places and the dominant mass of the castle which overlooks them. The covered yarn market, supported on stone pillars, was built in the seventeenth century, but there was a market place on the same site for centuries before that. Most of Dunster's history was linked with the Luttrell family, who have maintained their tenure of the castle from the Middle Ages to the present day. The castle itself was originally a Norman fortress but was razed during a revolt against King Stephen. There are still fragments of the later castle which was built in the thirteenth century, though most of modern Dunster belongs to two rebuildings, one carried out in Elizabethan times and the other in the eighteenth century. During the great English woollen boom of the fifteenth and sixteenth centuries more Somerset cloth passed through Dunster market than through any other market of the West Country and "dunsters" fetched a higher price than cloth marketed in other West Country centres. Today, though Dunster has slipped back almost into medieval quiet, it is thronged with visitors in summer from Minehead and other resorts.

117

## BASKET WEAVING IN WEST COUNTRY VILLAGES

THIS photograph was taken in Braunton, Devon. It could just as well have been in any of a score of villages in the lowlands of the West Country. The rude whitewashed cottages with their thatched roofs are found all over Devon and Somerset, especially in the countryside to the south of the Mendips. Reed beds supply the raw material for the roof thatches, and riverside willows that for the basket making. It is said that basket weaving as a rural industry is dying out. It has flourished at Braunton for nearly a thousand years, but there is a shortage of young recruits to enter the industry. Most of those engaged in it today are past middle age. The average age of the workers in one rural factory is over fifty-five. In ten years' time the industry may be dead for no other reason than dearth of workers, though there are other difficulties as well. For instance, materials cost much more now. Before 1939 a bundle of willow was priced at 8s. 6d. Today the price is nearly 25s. The result is that a rustic basket for which there used to be a ready market for bazaars and sales of work locally at about 1s. each now costs 4s. 6d., a price at which the craft products cannot compete with the specialized mass-produced products of urban factories. Even before the war foreign competition was a real worry to the rural craftsmen. With a return to free imports the rural industry may be swamped. Whatever its prospects, this country craft, like the more famous weaving of wool in Scotland's western isles, is still very much alive and its products contribute a modest addition to Britain's exports to dollar countries.

## PORTS OF SOUTH CORNWALL

CHINA-CLAY and tin are the traditional sources of the Duchy of Cornwall's wealth; the former still important, the latter now mined only in a very few places. St. Austell is the commercial centre of the china-clay industry, Helston is a former centre of tin mining. The pictures on this page are of the ports which serve these places: Charlestown (*left*), the port of St. Austell; Porthleven (*below*), the port of Helston. As a port, Porthleven has declined, but it is increasingly popular as a holiday resort and maintains its old prosperity. Charlestown, by contrast, is still an active port. In the photograph men are turning the capstan which works the lock gates.

## ON THE LIZARD'S EAST COAST

RIGHT off the beaten track and approached from inland only by a narrow, precipitous road which discourages visitors, Porthallow, photographed here, remains to a greater extent than any other Cornish village the typical fishing village as it was before the advent of the motor-car and twentieth-century development. There is no other industry in Porthallow today but fishing. The cottages in the upper terrace are still approached only by steep stone steps. Not a single new dwelling has been built within living memory in this charming group which faces the strand and the shelving cobble-beach. The fishing-boats are still pulled clear of the tide by the traditional type of pulley, of which two are seen in the foreground. If there are any summer visitors they are friends visiting friends, for catering for holiday-makers, the stand-by of most modern Cornish towns and villages, has never been embraced by the people of Porthallow. The beach on a bright summer's day, in contrast with the crowded beaches of other south-coast places, presents an appearance almost as deserted as in the quiet grey days of winter. Rough tracks lead along the coast in both directions from Porthallow, northward toward the estuary of the Helford and southward over a bold headland to Porthoustock, where there is a road leading to St. Keverne.

## IN AND AROUND POLPERRO

POLPERRO is one of the most beautiful of the Cornish fishing villages which have been
"discovered," though expansion has happily been limited here by its position in a narrow
defile through which a tiny river rushes to the sea, hemmed in on either side by cliff sides
too steep for modern building on the grand scale. The picture above shows how much
has been achieved. So quaintly placed are the modern villas clinging precariously to the cliff
side that in a comparatively few years they have become part of the scene and no longer
offend the eye. Even so, the chief fascination of the place is in the tiny harbour with its
array of fishing-boats and in the old-world cottages which are closely packed around it.
A mile or two inland where the hills still rise steeply from the narrow valley there are a few
farmhouses like the one pictured opposite, an old mill whose power was derived from Polperro's rivulet; now with its brightly whitewashed façade and trim cottages it is a model
of rural building unusual in a county whose farmhouses are generally built in a style
far more austere and less colourful than those of most other parts of southern England.

## MEVAGISSEY, THE PAST

TRADITION dies hard in Cornish fishing villages, and Mevagissey with its narrow streets (*left*) and its fishing harbour (*below*) clings to established custom with courage and determination. The narrow streets of the old town are unchanged and are here seen decorated for the annual carnival which attracts thousands of visitors into the narrow confines of this stronghold of the past. When the fishing-boats come into harbour they are swooped on by hundreds of gulls attracted by the smell and sight of fish. While the fishermen are unloading they direct the stream from a hose into the air to keep off the hungry birds, an expedient as effective as it is simple. Curious onlookers watch the efforts of the screaming birds to snatch their prey in the lee of the hose.

## MEVAGISSEY, THE PRESENT

THE spirit of Cornish conservatism is reflected in the pictures on the page opposite. The photograph above of the modern harbour and the new dwelling-places which have been built along the cliff road and inland from the crowded centre of old Mevagissey reflects equally the enterprise of the people of Mevagissey. Today the harbour is one of the finest of the small Cornish fishing ports, the outer harbour large enough to accommodate the most modern fishing vessels. Once famous for its pilchard fisheries, Mevagissey was one of the first to develop a canning industry so that none of the great catches of pilchards was wasted. When pilchards ceased to be the mainstay of Cornish fishing the Mevagissey fleet quickly adapted itself to less specialized fisheries. Today there is a quiet prosperity in this ancient Celtic settlement; fishing and catering for holiday-makers are the twin "industries" which assure the future. Though carnival week is the great event of the year, Mevagissey's streets are thronged by sightseers and other visitors through all the summer months.

## PORT ISAAC

PORT ISAAC, shown in both the photographs on this page, is set in a narrow gap between the cliffs on Cornwall's stormy north coast. It combines the beauty of old cottages with the interest of a tiny port; its setting is in scenery unsurpassed in Cornwall. The name is a corruption of Celtic words meaning "corn port," recalling the time long before railways had come to Britain when the small ports around the coast enjoyed a real and lasting prosperity from their shipping, which was the only means of communication between one part of the Duchy and another. As a port Port Isaac has declined like all its neighbours, though slate from the Delabole quarries has been shipped for nearly a century and still provides trade.

## IN THE TOE OF CORNWALL

Zennor (*right*) is one of the few inland villages in the toe of Cornwall. It is just off the road from St. Ives to Land's End. The road to the church is guarded by a great slab of stone, seen in the right foreground, a Logan stone which is a natural formation. The "mermaid of Zennor" which figures in many legends is said to have been attracted from the sea by the singing of one of the young men of Zennor. She disguised herself as a human being and finally persuaded the young man to jump with her off the near-by cliffs into the sea. Sennen Cove (*below*) is the nearest village to Land's End and is famous as one of the last places at which the fishing community used a net drawn across the cove and operated communally.

# INDEX

*Numbers in italics indicate illustrations*

*First published* 1951
*Made and printed in Great Britain by Odhams (Watford) Ltd., Watford*
*Copyright* T.651.R